Especially for

_____

From

_____

Date

_____

Written and compiled by Todd Hafer in association with Snapdragon Group℠, Tulsa, OK.

ISBN 978-1-61626-226-6

Published by Barbour Publishing, Inc., P.O. Box 719, Uhrichsville, Ohio 44683, www.barbourbooks.com

Our mission is to publish and distribute inspirational products offering exceptional value and biblical encouragement to the masses.

Member of the
Evangelical Christian
Publishers Association

Printed in China.

FUN FACTS FOR RACING FANS

BARBOUR
PUBLISHING

If everything is under control,
you are going too slow.

MARIO ANDRETTI

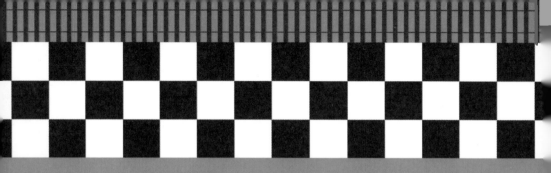

Bobby Isaac, one of NASCAR's early stars, was so poor as a child that he didn't own a pair of shoes until age 13. He dropped out of school in sixth grade and worked racking balls at a pool hall before turning to professional racing.

From 1976 to 1978, Cale Yarborough won three consecutive NASCAR Sprint Cup Series championships, becoming the first driver to accomplish the feat. It would take 20 years before another driver (Jimmie Johnson) would match Yarborough's trifecta.

Actor Robert Duvall turned down a role in a *Godfather* sequel so that he could play a crew chief in the 1990 hit movie *Days of Thunder*, starring Tom Cruise.

At the 1965 Southern 500 at Darlington, Ned Jarrett beat runner-up Buck Baker by an incredible 14 laps. (Fourteen laps equal 19.25 miles.)

NASCAR was founded in 1947 by Bill France Sr., a racer himself, with the aim to draw bigger crowds to racing events, secure more prize money for drivers, and institute safety measures.

During their careers, NASCAR legends Richard Petty and David Pearson raced against each other 550 times. Petty bested Pearson, 289 to 261. (In 63 of their races, they finished 1-2.)

On November 9, 1813, Andrew Jackson led 2,000 troops into eastern Alabama to expel the area of the Creek Indians. According to legend, a Creek medicine man placed a curse on the area as he was marched away. That land is now occupied by the Talladega Superspeedway.

The 2004 Chase for the NASCAR NEXTEL Cup was one of the most exciting in history, as Kurt Busch finished fifth to edge Jimmie Johnson by just eight points to win the overall championship.

After Ronald Reagan watched Richard Petty win the 1984 Firecracker 400 at Daytona Beach, the President and the King sat down to enjoy a bucket of Kentucky Fried Chicken at a picnic held in a Victory Lane garage. During the meal, Petty told Reagan, who was up for reelection, "I won my race. Now you go and win yours."

The race is not always to the swift,
nor the battle to the strong,
but that's the way to bet.

DAMON RUNYAN

The Oldsmobile 88, with its Rocket V-8 engine, dominated NASCAR's early days (the late 1940s and early 1950s), eventually giving way to the flathead six of the Hudson Hornet.

The huge "Banquet 400" logo that sits on the infield grass along the Kansas Speedway's front stretch is nearly the size of a football field.

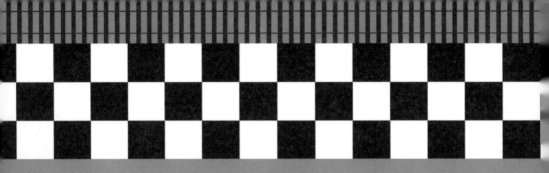

On November 15, 1992, 55-year-old Richard Petty finished his 1,185th race, the Hooters 500. As he limped his wrecked car along its final lap (at 40 mph), the crowd at the Atlanta Motor Speedway gave him a track-shaking ovation.

At age 23, Jeff Gordon became the first man to win at the Indianapolis Motor Speedway in a stock car (at the inaugural Brickyard 400). More than 350,000 fans watched the historic victory.

In the early 1900s, electric cars accounted for 38 percent of all vehicle sales in the United States. However, a race featuring these cars would have been rather mundane. Most topped out at just 20 miles per hour.

Midway through the 1970 season, NASCAR mandated that all cars use a restrictor plate—to limit the amount of air/fuel mixture going into the cylinders, thus reducing horsepower and top speeds.

In stock-car racing's early days, many drivers competed in slacks and T-shirts. Many didn't wear helmets or seat belts, and prize money was often less than $100 per race.

In 2005 the NASCAR Nationwide Series raced at Mexico City's famous Autodromo Hermanos Rodriguez road course, marking the first time a NASCAR points race was held outside of the United States.

NASCAR vehicles do sport several interior gauges. However, neither a speedometer nor an odometer can be found on a NASCAR dashboard. (Drivers judge their speed using the tachometer, which shows revolutions per minute.)

*Cast all your anxiety on him
because he cares for you.*

I PETER 5:7

On a typical race weekend, a NASCAR team uses between 9 and 14 sets of tires. (The treadless tires cost about $400 each.)

Many of stock-car racing's early star drivers—such as Junior Johnson and Glenn Dunnaway—honed their navigational skills by running moonshine on back-country roads.

NASCAR drivers cannot take bathroom breaks during races, which often extend to more than three hours. However, they sweat so much that "holding it" typically isn't a problem. (During a race, a driver can lose up to 10 pounds, almost all of it water.)

The year 1971 was the first that saw all NASCAR races run on pavement, although many drivers continued to compete on local dirt tracks throughout the 1970s.

Endurance and strength are important for NASCAR drivers, who must pilot their cars for more than three hours at a time—in the 120-degree heat that builds up inside their vehicles. That's why many drivers, like Mark Martin, work out every day, even the day after a race.

At just 21 years of age, Kyle Busch won
two races in his first NASCAR NEXTEL
Cup season, becoming the youngest
driver to win a pole and a race.

On October 15, 1997, Royal Air Force pilot Andy Green broke the sound barrier (and set the world's first supersonic speed record on land) in Nevada's Black Rock Desert. Driving a Thrust SSC car built by Richard Noble, Green recorded two runs at an average speed of 763.035 mph. (The speed of sound for that place and time: 751.251.)

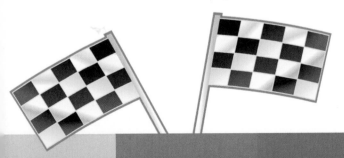

In his two-decade career, Bobby Allison won **85** NASCAR races, placing him third in the all-time rankings. However, a NASCAR season championship eluded him.

Buck Baker, one of NASCAR's pioneering drivers, won 46 races in 636 starts. (He was even more successful in post-race fistfights, where, according to his son Buddy, he never lost.)

A good pit crew is invaluable, and that's why, many times, they're the first team members I mention when I climb out of my car in Victory Lane.

MARK MARTIN

Darlington Raceway's egg shape—with tight turns one and two—has earned it the nickname "The Track Too Tough to Tame." Built in 1950, Darlington is also NASCAR's original superspeedway.

In a 1999 race, Tony Stewart forgot
to put on his heat shields over his boots.
He ended up with burns and blisters
on his heels and couldn't race for
more than a week.

A stock car has no glass; that means no headlights,
taillights, or (typically) side windows.
(The front and rear windows are made of Lexan,
a hard, shatterproof plastic.)

The Ford Mustang, introduced in 1964,
quickly became a favorite with car buyers.
The Mustang was the first compact
car to feature sporty styling.

The front and rear wings on Formula One cars aren't there for decoration. The wings produce a down-force that presses the cars to the ground, making them easier and safer to maneuver.

In the middle of a 1973 race at Talladega, lead driver Bobby Isaac pulled off the track, climbed from his car, and walked away. He claimed a voice told him to do so.

One of NASCAR's earliest racing venues, the circular Langhorne Speedway lacked a single straightaway. The Pennsylvania track hosted its last NASCAR race in 1957. The site is now home to a shopping center.

In the 1970s, David Pearson and Richard Petty combined to win 136 races. In the 1980s, they won just 11—and none of those came after 1984.

In 1978 a California real-estate developer paid $5,000 to enter a local driver in a stock-car race. The driver was a virtually penniless high school dropout with a bad reputation. His name was Dale Earnhardt. Just one year later, Earnhardt won his first major NASCAR race, the Southeastern 500 at Bristol.

One thing I promised myself is that I would retire while I was at the top. I didn't want to go out while on my way down.

NED JARRETT,
AFTER RETIRING IN 1966,
WITH 50 WINS TO HIS CREDIT

By the year 1972, A. J. Foyt had already won three Indianapolis 500s, five IndyCar championships, the 24 Hours of LeMans, and the Daytona 500. "There's a lot of us glad A.J. doesn't come down here full-time," Richard Petty told reporters after Foyt's win at the 1972 Daytona 500. "There might not be any races left for us to win."

Before the 1971 NASCAR season, the R. J. Reynolds Tobacco Company posted $100,000 in year-end bonus money and plastered its red Winston cigarette logo on racetracks, race cars, and sports pages nationwide. (Reynolds' NASCAR sponsorship allowed it to bypass the famous government-issued ban on TV advertising for cigarettes.)

Ray Harroun won the first Indianapolis 500 in 1911.
His average speed: just 74.59 mph.

The most famous endurance auto race is the grueling 24 Hours of LeMans, held annually in LeMans, France. Typically, teams of three drivers share the duties behind the wheel.

On March 24, 1970, Buddy Baker set a world-record 200.447 mph for a single lap on a closed course, earning him the nickname Mr. 200 Miles. Baker set the mark at Talladega, in his Cotton Owens–prepared Dodge Daytona.

After a 1994 crash, Ernie Irvan survived an emergency tracheotomy, a coma, pneumonia, swelling of the brain, and an aneurysm. He returned to racing just over a year later, finishing sixth his first time back on the track.

Early in his successful racing career,
Junior Johnson was nabbed by federal agents
for running moonshine, resulting in an unplanned
11-month absence from the sport.

Ronald Reagan was the first sitting U.S. president to attend a NASCAR event. Reagan picked a good race, as he saw Richard Petty win his 200th race at the 1984 Firecracker 400.

While Formula One Grand Prix cars can exceed 200 mph on straightaways, drivers often have to slow to speeds of about 30 mph to negotiate the sharp turns offered by some courses.

You will keep in perfect peace him whose mind is steadfast, because he trusts in you. Trust in the LORD forever, for the LORD, the LORD, is the Rock eternal.

ISAIAH 26:3-4

Dale Jarrett's win at the 1993 Daytona 500 gave Joe Gibbs (a former Super Bowl champion football coach) his first win as a NASCAR racing-team owner.

The 2005 Aaron's 449 at Talladega is best known for "The Big One," a 25-car pileup that took 43 minutes to clean up. However, all but four of the affected cars managed to return to the race. Jeff Gordon took the checkered flag.

On February 26, 1967, Mario Andretti stunned the racing world by winning the ninth Daytona 500. (Andretti was known as an open-wheel specialist, and some stock-car experts questioned his ability to master the bigger cars.) But Andretti built a huge lead that allowed him to win—despite running out of gas at one point in the race.

After Dale Earnhardt's tragic death at the 2001 Daytona 500, the racing community honored him throughout the season with a silent third lap (Earnhardt's car was number 3). When Kevin Harvick (Earnhardt's replacement that year) won his first race, he circled the track in reverse direction, extending three fingers out the driver's side window.

Little Joe Weatherly, a NASCAR star of the early 1960s, was known to steal competitors' car keys or put drugs in their water bottles in order to gain a competitive advantage. Known as the Clown Prince of Racing, Weatherly drove to 25 victories. (He was killed in a 1964 crash at the Motor Trend 500 at Riverside International Raceway.)

The last dirt-track race for NASCAR's top series was the Home State 200, contested September, 30, 1970, on a one-mile track at Raleigh, North Carolina's State Fairgrounds Speedway. Richard Petty won the race.

At 1.54 miles, the Atlanta Motor Speedway track is one of the longest (and fastest) on the NASCAR circuit. Incidentally, the track's grandstands accommodate 124,000 fans.

The Indianapolis Motor Speedway boasts the most grandstand seating of any track on the NASCAR circuit, with accommodations for more than a quarter of a million fans.

Racing is truly in the Petty family's blood. Richard Petty's grandfather died at age 98—after floorboarding his Ford Model T on a North Carolina back road.

Let's get one thing straight:
Richard Petty is still the King. I'm just
happy to be mentioned with him.

DALE EARNHARDT, ON HIS LONGTIME RIVAL

Peter De Paolo, winner of the 1925 Indy 500, was the first driver to average above 100 mph for the race. De Paolo averaged 101.13 mph during his victory. Incidentally, it would take five years before another Indy winner cracked the 100 mph–average barrier.

Darlington Raceway opened its gates in 1950. The track was the longtime host of the Southern 500, the first of NASCAR's 500-mile races.

Hot-rodder Warren "The Professor" Johnson has maintained his driving prowess, even at an age when many people retire. In 2010 the 66-year-old, six-time NHRA champion was still winning races.

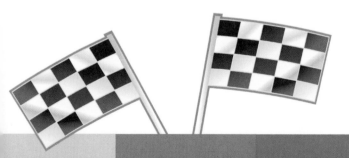

At the 1987 Daytona 500, Bill Elliott posted a qualifying speed of 210.364 miles per hour. (Because of high speeds like this, in 1988 NASCAR began requiring cars to run restrictor plates for Daytona races.)

Dale Jarrett is one of NASCAR's finest all-around athletes. In high school, he starred in football, basketball, and baseball. And he was offered a full-ride golf scholarship to the University of North Carolina. (He didn't begin racing cars until age 20.)

Before racing stock cars, Casey Mears raced BMX bicycles (starting at age 4), ATVs, go-karts, and SuperLites.

Mario Andretti is the last driver from the United States to earn a Formula One World Grand Prix Championship. Andretti claimed the title in 1978, becoming the second-ever U.S. driver to achieve the feat.

Because of its steep 36-degree banking, the half-mile oval at the Bristol Motor Speedway is nicknamed "The Toilet Bowl."

As a child, Mario Andretti, winner of both Grand Prix and stock-car championships, spent more than three years in a displaced persons camp after World War II. (Andretti was born in Trieste, a city on the Adriatic Sea.)

We will always be indebted to Winston for what they did for the sport. But as long as we were connected to cigarettes, there was going to be a stigma.

JEFF GORDON, ON NASCAR'S PRIMARY-SPONSOR SWITCH FROM R. J. REYNOLDS TO NEXTEL (WHICH WAS LATER PURCHASED BY SPRINT)

In 2003 Sunoco signed a 10-year contract with NASCAR, making Sunoco gasoline the sport's official fuel.

NASCAR mandated the use of the HANS (Head and Neck Support) Device on October 17, 2001. The device limits the forward motion of a driver's head in the event of a crash.

At the 2001 Cracker Barrel 500, Kevin Harvick nipped Jeff Gordon in a 190-mph drag race to the finish line. Harvick's margin of victory was a scant 20 inches.

The 1950 Southern 500 at Darlington was the first stock-car race held on a superspeedway. Hollywood stuntman Johnny "Madman" Mantz won the event in a lightweight Plymouth—fitted with bulky truck tires. Mantz bested a field of veteran NASCAR regulars who suffered frequent blowouts on the high-banked turns. Meanwhile, Mantz's tires held up for the entire race and never had to be changed.

Racing legend Red Byron interrupted his stock-car career to fly 58 missions as a B-52 tail gunner in World War II. His leg was mangled when his plane was shot down in 1943. But when NASCAR held its first officially sanctioned race at Daytona Beach in 1948, Byron was there to win it, beating the likes of Fireball Roberts, Fonty Flock, and Marshall Teague.

In the mid-1930s, Bill France's stock-car races at Daytona Beach prompted fierce protests from local churches, who questioned the godliness of driving family-style cars at breakneck speeds on Sunday afternoons.

Racing star Danica Patrick, the best-ever female finisher at the Indianapolis 500 (third in 2009) has also been featured twice in *Sports Illustrated*'s annual swimsuit issue.

Nextel became NASCAR's primary sponsor before the 2004 season, replacing R. J. Reynolds (Winston), which had become the series' first major sponsor in 1971.

During an average NASCAR race at Talladega, about 12,000 pounds of hot dogs are served. (If those dogs were laid end to end, they would circle the 2.66-mile track, with another .14 miles worth of hot dogs to spare.)

With all your heart you must trust the LORD and not your own judgment. Always let him lead you, and he will clear the road for you to follow.

PROVERBS 3:5–6 CEV

When Richard Petty retired after 35 years
of racing (on November 15, 1992), he had
amassed 555 top-5 finishes in 1,185 starts.

In 1991, 55-year-old Harry Gant earned the nickname "Mr. September" after he won four consecutive races in the ninth month of the year.

Originally known as Charlotte Motor Speedway, the Concord, North Carolina, oval became Lowe's Motor Speedway in 1999, making it the first track to be named after a corporate sponsor.

In NASCAR racing, a white flag has nothing to do with surrender. It simply means that only one lap remains in a race.

NASCAR Radio debuted on XM Satellite Radio on September 25, 2001, making NASCAR racing the first to boast a 24-hour radio station dedicated to a single sport.

Eastern Pennsylvania's Pocono Raceway is the only NASCAR track with a distinctive triangular shape. Each of the 2.5-mile raceway's corners offers a different turning radius and banking angle, making it a unique challenge for drivers—and chassis tuners!

Several top drivers boycotted the first running of the Talladega 500, questioning whether their tires could withstand the Talladega Speedway's plus-200 mph speeds.

Western New York's Watkins Glen International is one of just two NASCAR road courses. The Glen's 2.45 miles offer 11 turns.

During a race, a black flag warns a driver to pull into the pits, either because the car is damaged or he or she is being penalized for a rules infraction.

The name Penske is as closely associated
with car racing as the wheel.

ROGER PENSKE

From an aerial view, the elongated Martinsville Speedway track looks just like a paperclip. Opened in 1949, The Paperclip is the oldest track still hosting NASCAR races today.

During his **26**-year NASCAR career, the legendary Dale Earnhardt won more than **$42** million in prize money. He posted **76** wins, **281** top-5 performances, and finished in the top **10** an amazing **428** times.

Jeff Gordon was only 24 when he won his first NASCAR championship (in 1995), making him the organization's second-youngest champ.

A NASCAR pit crew can provide 22 gallons of gas, replace four tires, and clean a windshield in under 18 seconds.

When title sponsor Nextel signed its
10-year agreement with NASCAR in 2004,
the deal was valued at $750 million.

Red Byron, who won NASCAR's first Strictly Stock title in 1949, first drove an automobile at age five and owned his first car (a Model T Ford) at ten. He raced that car on a homemade track carved out of a cow pasture.

Open-wheel cars (such as Formula One) have open cockpits and no fenders, so they can't bump and jockey with competitor vehicles, as stock cars do.

At age 16, Danica Patrick dropped out of high school to race Indy-style cars overseas in England's Formula Vauxhall Series.

The 1990 Daytona 500 was memorable
for Dale Earnhardt—but not in a good way.
He led for 155 of the race's 200 laps but
lost when he blew a tire in the last mile.

My dad used to prop me up on his lap and make me take the steering wheel. Then he'd slam his foot on the accelerator, and off we'd go. I was stuck steering the car at speeds over 80 miles an hour on gravel roads. The more we drove, the more I got used to it—and the more I fell in love with the sensation.

MARK MARTIN

Edward "Fireball" Roberts didn't get his famous nickname for his fearless driving. "Fireball" referred to his prowess as a hard-throwing baseball pitcher.

Auto racing, bull fighting, and mountain climbing are the only real sports. . . all others are games.

ERNEST HEMINGWAY

At age 57, legendary driver Buck Baker made a surprise comeback at the 1976 Dixie 500. He qualified 13th and went on to finish a very respectable 6th.

At age 59, John Force won his 1,000th career funny-car victory, at the 2008 NHRA Nationals. Now in his 60s, Force continues to be competitive on the NHRA scene.

In his 15-year career, Lee Petty finished in the top ten 332 times in 427 career NASCAR starts. (Lee is the father of Richard Petty, the grandfather of Kyle Petty.)

During the 1967 season, Richard Petty won 10 consecutive races, on his way to 27 total wins. Both totals are considered by some racing experts to be unbreakable records—like Cal Ripken's consecutive-games streak in baseball.

Rex White, who won 28 races in his
brief stock-car career, stood only five feet,
four inches tall and tipped the scales at 135
pounds. (He was stricken with polio as a child.)

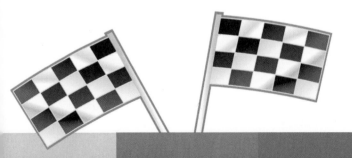

Las Vegas Motor Speedway sees lots of action beyond its use as a NASCAR track. Local drag racers run there every week, and the local police department often reserves the 1.5-mile track for driver training.

In 1978 President Jimmy Carter
acknowledged NASCAR's growing popularity
by inviting drivers to the White House.

"Be strong and courageous. Do not be terrified; do not be discouraged, for the LORD your God will be with you wherever you go."

JOSHUA 1:9

On February 18, 1979, CBS Sports carried the first flag-to-flag coverage of a NASCAR event, the Daytona 500. Sixteen million TV viewers watched Richard Petty avoid bumping between Cale Yarborough and Donnie Allison to slip to victory on the last lap.

Moonshine runner turned NASCAR driver Junior Johnson caught the attention of famous writer Tom Wolfe, who profiled Johnson in the March 1965 issue of *Esquire* magazine. The title of Wolfe's piece: "The Last American Hero."

In 1977 Janet Guthrie became the first woman to qualify for the Daytona 500. She ended up finishing a respectable 12th.

On Valentine's Day of 1988,
Bobby Allison and his son Davey
finished 1-2 in the Daytona 500.

April 29, 1982, was an historic day for NASCAR.
At Talladega, Benny Parsons posted a qualifying
lap of over 200 mph, a first for the sport.

NASCAR ran its first official race, on Daytona's beach-road course, on February 15, 1948. Red Byron piloted his Ford to victory.

In NASCAR, the "hat dance" has nothing to do with dancing. The term refers to a race winner's standing in Victory Lane and donning dozens of baseball caps adorned with various sponsors' logos. Photographers snap pictures to send or sell to each sponsor.

The Martinsville Speedway is NASCAR's smallest track, at just .526 miles. The oval was built in 1947, meaning it actually pre-dates NASCAR itself.

Aerodynamics is for those who
cannot manufacture good engines.

ENZO FERRARI

I knew I was in trouble when I saw grass, because I know there ain't no grass on a racetrack.

CALE YARBOROUGH, AFTER SAILING OVER A GUARDRAIL AT DARLINGTON AND HITTING A TELEPHONE POLE (HE WALKED AWAY UNINJURED.)

The "Kissing of the Bricks" is a ritual traditionally performed by the winning team of the Brickyard 400. (In 2005 the race was renamed the Allstate 400 at the Brickyard.)

The first-ever Daytona 500 entertained almost 42,000 spectators, who packed the grandstands—and the infield—to see Lee Petty edge Johnny Beauchamp in a photo finish. The race was so close that it took officials 61 hours to study film footage and still photos and declare Petty's victory.

We drove for the sheer fun of driving because there wasn't that much money to be made.

RICHARD PETTY

Glenn Dunnaway won the inaugural Strictly Stock Race on June 19, 1949. Dunnaway's 1947 bootlegger Ford bested Jim Roper's Lincoln, earning the winning driver $2,000.

The air guns used in big-time auto racing allow
the front- and rear-tire changers to remove
five lug nuts in less than two seconds.

June 13, 1954, saw NASCAR drivers tackle their first road course, a two-mile, five-turn course on the concrete runways and taxiways of the Linden, New Jersey, airport. (New Yorker Al Keller, a part-time driver, won the race in a lightweight Jaguar.)

In a 1956 race at Daytona Beach, Russ Truelove's Mercury hit a soft patch in the sand and flipped almost a dozen times. Truelove walked away from the accident, exiting his smoking car via the passenger door.

Graham Rahal is the youngest winner in the history of major open-wheel racing. At just 19, he won his debut IndyCar Series race—the Grand Prix of St. Petersburg. But longtime fans of the sport weren't that surprised. Graham's father is racing great Bobby Rahal.

After winning the 1972 Wilkes 400, Richard Petty was attacked by a drunken fan in Victory Lane. Order was restored when Petty's brother Maurice used Richard's helmet to smack the drunk on the head.

It's just another number, but it's a big one. I figured I'd eventually get there, but as hard as they've gotten to be, I didn't know when.

RICHARD PETTY,
ON HIS 200TH WIN (THE 1984 FIRECRACKER 400 AT DAYTONA)

The 1973 running of the Winston 500 featured
a 21-car crash along the backstretch of lap 11.
Only 26 cars (60 started) were running at the end
of the race, which was won by David Pearson.

At Talladega in 1993, Dale Earnhardt edged Ernie Irvan by just .005 seconds, the closest finish since NASCAR installed its computerized verification system.

On April 2, 2000, 19-year-old Adam Petty made his Winston Cup debut in the DIRECTV 500, making him America's first fourth-generation professional athlete. Adam's great-grandfather Lee watched the race on TV, just three days before he passed away, at age 86.

Canadian dirt-track ace Milt Marion won $1,000 for winning the first major stock-car race at Daytona Beach (on March 8, 1936). The race drew about 20,000 fans, most of whom bypassed ticket booths and marched over sand dunes to view the event.

From the year 2000 to 2004, Germany's Michael Schumacher won five consecutive Formula One Grand Prix world championships.

Jackie Smith won the inaugural Volunteer 500 at Bristol in 1961. Smith, driving a Pontiac, averaged just 68.37 mph on his way to victory.

In 1958 Shorty Rollins became NASCAR's first official Rookie of the Year. Others to have won the honor include Richard Petty, Dale Earnhardt, Donnie and Davey Allison, Jeff Gordon, and Tony Stewart.

The winner ain't the one with the fastest car, it's the one who refuses to lose.

DALE EARNHARDT

In 1906 the world one-mile land speed record was held by a steam-powered Stanley automobile. The Stanley's record speed was 127.659 mph.

A good name is to be chosen rather than great riches, loving favor rather than silver and gold.

PROVERBS 22:1 NKJV

In what other sport do you get a 15-second break every hour?

DALE EARNHARDT SR.
ON THE "DRIVERS AREN'T ATHLETES" DEBATE

Darlington Raceway hosted the NASCAR series'
first 500-mile race, the Southern 500, on
September 4, 1950. The race started a field of 75
drivers and took more than six hours to complete.
Johnny "Madman" Mantz drove his Plymouth to victory.

Age 50 was good to NASCAR legend Bobby Allison.
He won the Daytona 500 during that milestone year,
although he had to hold off a late charge
from his son Davey to do it.

In 1949 Red Byron became NASCAR's first Strictly Stock Series champ. Byron earned $5,800 for two wins in six starts.

The final NASCAR race to be held on Daytona's
beach course was run on February 23, 1958.
Paul Goldsmith claimed the historic victory.

In 1958 Florida sportswriters voted Fireball Roberts as Professional Athlete of the Year. This marked the first time the honor went to a race-car driver.

On December 1, 1963, Wendell Scott became the first African-American to win a premier-division NASCAR race, beating Buck Baker at Jacksonville Speedway.

I go race to race to race, and that's how I've always done it. I focus as much as I can on the upcoming weekend, and when we leave, I start focusing on the next race. Maybe I have a one-track mind.

JEFF GORDON

Though it has become a word in its own right,
"NASCAR" is an acronym that stands for
National Association for Stock Car Auto Racing.

It's one thing to have fan support when you're riding high. It's another thing to have it during the rough times.

DALE EARNHARDT JR.

The famous Indianapolis 500 open-wheel race saw its first running in 1911, at the legendary Indianapolis Motor Speedway (which was originally paved with bricks).

For us there is no difference between second and tenth, it's win or nothing.

DENNY HAMLIN

Desire is the key to motivation, but it's determination and commitment to an unrelenting pursuit of your goal—a commitment to excellence—that will enable you to attain the success you seek.

MARIO ANDRETTI

Speed is relative. Does it feel fast going 70 miles per hour down an eight-lane highway? No, probably not, but I bet it does if you are going down some single-lane dirt road. It's the same in a race car. It depends on the track.

KYLE PETTY

It took NASCAR driving prodigy Joey Logano only three races to win his first major title. He earned his first Nationwide Series victory at age 18.

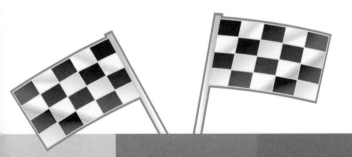

Assigned to cover the 1933 Indy 500, a Denver sportswriter called his newspaper and promised, "Will overhead winner"—meaning he would send the winner's name via the overhead telegraph wires when the race was complete. His editor, unfortunately, misunderstood, thinking that a driver named Will Overhead had captured the race. The headline the next morning in the *World Independent* newspaper: "OVERHEAD WINS INDIANAPOLIS RACE."

The newest NASCAR track, the Kansas Speedway, opened its gates in June of 2001 and hosted its first NASCAR NEXTEL Cup race less than four months later. This track is one of the circuit's safest, as 1.28 of its 1.5 miles feature the high-tech SAFER (Steel and Foam Energy Reduction) barrier.

When you're racing, you aren't thinking
about making history; you're just thinking
about winning races and championships.

RUSTY WALLACE

If someone could design a race car that could run on methane, the daily flatulence of a single sheep could power that car for 25 miles.

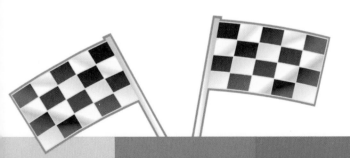

Good drivers have great seasons. But the truly great drivers have eras. Ladies and gentlemen, this is the Jeff Gordon Era.

DARRELL WALTRIP (IN 1998)

Auto racing is boring except when a car is going
at least 172 miles per hour upside down.

DAVE BARRY

Henry Ford's 1908 Model T car, the first
mass-produced automobile, carried a
retail price of $850. Between 1908 and
1928, Ford's company produced 20 million
Model Ts, some of which were used
in early auto races.

Many NASCAR fans know that in 1967, Richard Petty notched 27 victories in a single season, including 10 straight. However, he set yet another record in '67 by claiming 15 of those victories from pole position.

In the movie *Back to the Future*, the device that transported Marty McFly back and forth in time was originally supposed to be a refrigerator. However, filmmakers changed the portal of choice to a DeLorean sports car, after someone raised a concern that the film would encourage young children to play in refrigerators.

The current version of the *Hunters for the Hungry* venison cookbook contains recipes from NASCAR drivers Ward Burton, John Andretti, and Dick Trickle.

You win some, lose some,
and wreck some.

DALE EARNHARDT SR.

In a long race, the temperature inside a stock-car driver's suit can exceed 120 degrees. On very hot days, the men and women who occupy the costumes of theme-park characters like Goofy and Donald Duck endure the same extremes.

On March 24, 1970, Buddy Baker made NASCAR history by becoming the organization's first driver to post a test-speed run faster than 200 mph (at Talladega). (Baker's effort was also a world record.)

Italy's Giuseppe Farina was the first Grand Prix world champion, winning the title in 1950.

Thy word is a lamp unto my feet,
and a light unto my path.

Psalm 119:105 KJV

Before Marc Gene, David Brabham, and Alexander Wurz won the 2009 24 Hours of LeMans in a diesel-powered Peugeot, Audi teams had won the previous five races, and eight of the last ten.

Brad Daugherty, the National Basketball Association's overall No. I draft pick in 1986, is an avid car-racing fan and frequent TV commentator and analyst for various races.

Birthday number 9 was a momentous one for Danica Patrick. She received a go-kart from her father and began racing around a makeshift oval—marked by paint cans—in the parking lot of Papa Patrick's glass store.

The Time Almanac places the invention of the wheel at around 3700 BC. But a rubber tire couldn't meet the road until much later. Rubber was invented in 1839.

At age 15, Alissa Geving became the youngest American female to win a full-size sprint car race, taking the checkered flag at a 25-lap race at Petaluma Speedway.

In 2009 Camping World became the new title sponsor for the NASCAR Truck Series, replacing Craftsman Tools.

Automobile racing originated in France back in 1894.
It debuted in the United States the following year.

The giant gas cans used by a stock-car pit crew's "gas man" weigh about 90 pounds when full. Most pit stops require two cans' worth of gas.

In mid-2010 IndyCar driver Davey Hamilton returned to racing at Fort Worth's Texas Motor Speedway, almost nine years after a horrific accident at that same track almost cost him both of his feet.

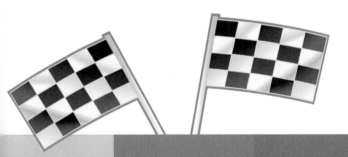

You want to win every race,
but sometimes you have to take
what the car is going to give you.

KURT "WILD MAN" BUSCH

Racing is a matter of spirit, not strength.

JANET GUTHRIE

At age 13, Logan Ruffin won three Crate/ASA Late Model Series auto races, becoming the youngest driver—and winner—in the event's 31-year history.

Stock-car tires weigh about 75 pounds each, and must be handled with extreme caution by a pit crew's front- and rear-tire carriers, as they become extremely hot during a race.

Former Super Bowl–winning football coach Joe Gibbs has also proven himself a keen auto racing mind. He signed future star driver Joey Logano to Joe Gibbs Racing when Logano was only 14.

The Batmobile featured in the 1960s TV show
Batman was built on the chassis of a Chevy Impala.

Harry Gant is NASCAR's oldest winner. He took the checkered flag at Michigan Speedway's Champion 400 at age 52.

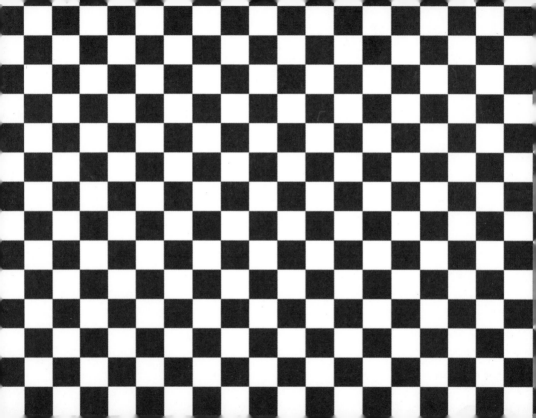